KIDS Sing Praise 3

32 *Action Songs of Praise, Scripture, and Sing-Along Fun*

ARRANGED AND TRANSCRIBED
BY LARRY MAYFIELD

FOREWORD...

When I began to compile songs for *Kids Sing Praise 3*, I was afraid that it might be difficult to find songs that matched the quality of *Kids Sing Praise 1 and 2.* It seemed that we used all the really great songs in the very first project!

To my surprise (and delight), I began to discover several wonderful new songs as well as many "classics" that we had somehow overlooked before. As a result of this search, the book you hold in your hands is probably one of the most delightful and spiritually significant collections of children's songs in years.

With every bit of the charm and sparkle of *Kids Sing Praise 1 and 2, Kids Sing Praise 3* is a singable, memorable collection of favorites - old and new. You'll recognize many of the songs from your childhood as well as songs from the best of today's writers of children's music. As your children sing these songs, they will be learning the unchangeable truth of God's word that will stay with them the rest of their lives!

We are excited about *Kids Sing Praise 3* and hope that you and your children will find it to be a blessing.

Ed Kee
Creative Director

Also Available:

Volume 1	Special Singer's Edition Songbook (43 Songs)	BK-3021
	Double Length Stereo Cassette	C-25073
	Double Length Split-Track Cassette	C-25027
	Kids Sing Praise Video, Volume 1 *(Featuring Songs from Kids Sing Praise, Volume 1)*	V-25027
Volume 2	Special Singer's Edition Songbook (35 Songs)	BK-3030
	Double Length Stereo Cassette	C-25071
	Double Length Split-Track Cassette	C-25064
	Kids Sing Praise Video, Volume 2 *(Featuring Songs from Kids Sing Praise, Volume 2)*	V-25071
	Spiral Bound Songbook (80 Songs, including songs on Volumes 1 and 2)	BK-3008
Volume 3	Double Length Stereo Cassette	C-5066N
	Double Length Split-Track Cassette	C-5159N

INDEX

I Am A "C"(H-R-I-S-T-I-A-N)

TRADITIONAL

9
E♭ E♭7/B♭ E♭7 E♭7/B♭ E♭7 E♭7/B♭ E♭7 E♭7/B♭
C - H - R - I - S - T in my H - E - A - R - T, And I will
11
E♭7 E♭7/B♭ E♭7 D♭/F E♭7/G A♭ A♭/E♭ A♭
L - I - V - E E - T - E - R - N - A - L - L - Y. I am a
13
A♭/E♭ A♭ A♭/E♭ A♭ A♭/E♭ A♭ A♭/E♭
C, I am a C - H, I am a
15
A♭ A♭/E♭ A♭ A♭6/C A♭m6/C♭ E♭7/B♭ E♭7 E♭7/B♭
C - H - R - I - S - T - I - A - N, And I have

17
Eb7 Eb7/Bb Eb7 Eb7/Bb Eb7 Eb7/Bb Eb7 Eb7/Bb
C - H - R - I - S - T in my H - E - A - R - T, And I will
19
Eb7 Eb7/Bb Eb7 Db/F Eb7/G
1.
Ab Ab/Eb Ab
L - I - V - E E - T - E - R - N - A - L - L - Y. I am a
21
2.
Ab Ab/Eb Ab Ab6/C Abm6/Cb Eb7/Bb Eb7 Eb7/Bb Eb7
N - A - L - L - Y. I have C - H - R - I - S - T in my
23
Eb7/Bb Eb7 Eb7/Bb Eb7 Eb7/Bb Eb7 Db/F Eb7/G Ab Ab/Eb Ab/C Ab
H - E - A - R - T, And I will L - I - V - E E - T - E - R - N - A - L - L - Y!

I'm Glad

Words and Music by
RUTH SCHRAM

15
Eb Ab Fm7 Bb Bb/D
Lord! I'm glad! (clap clap) I'm glad! (clap clap) I'm
Lord? Are you glad? (clap clap) Are you glad? (clap clap) Are you
18
Eb Ebmaj7 Ab Ab/Bb Eb
glad! (clap clap) I'm glad! (clap clap) I'm glad, I'm glad, I'm
glad? (clap clap) Are you glad? (clap clap) Are you glad, are you glad, are you
21
Bbm6/Db C7 Fm7 Bb7
1.
Eb Eb/Bb Eb Eb/Bb
glad! I'm glad He is my Lord!
glad? Are you glad He is your
25
Eb Eb/Bb Eb
Are you
2.
Eb Eb/Bb Eb Eb/Bb
Lord?

29 E♭ E♭/D B♭/C B♭/D C7/E F
I'm glad, I'm glad, I'm
glad, are you glad, are you
32 Am7 Dm7 Gm7 C7 F B♭/F C7
glad! I'm glad I'll live in heav - en! I'm
glad? Are you glad you'll live in heav - en? Are you
35 F Fmaj7 Am7 D7♭9 Gm7 C7
glad, I'm glad, I'm glad! I'm glad I'll live with
glad, are you glad, are you glad? Are you glad you'll live with
38 F Fsus/G F/A B♭ Gm7 C7 Gm7/D C7/E
Him! I'm glad! (clap clap) I'm glad! (clap clap) I'm
Him? Are you glad? (clap clap) Are you glad? (clap clap) Are you

41 F Am7 Bb Bb/C F
glad! (clap clap) I'm — glad! (clap clap) I'm — glad, I'm — glad, I'm —
glad? (clap clap) Are you glad? (clap clap) Are you glad, are you glad, are you
44 Am7 D7b9 Gm7 C7 1. F F/C F
glad! I'm — glad I'll live with Him! Are you
glad? Are you glad you'll live with
48 2. F F/A Bb Bb2/C F F/E Cm6/Eb D7 Gm7 Am7 Bb6 Gm7
Him? I'm glad, I'm glad, I'm glad! I'm glad I'll
52 Bbmaj7/C C C7 F F/C F F/C F/C F C7 F
live with Him!

Fill In The Blanks

Words by
DOTTIE RAMBO

Music by
DOTTIE RAMBO & DAVID HUNTSINGER

14 A F#m7 A B A/B
what do you think, He swal-lowed bro - ther (whoop!) as
16 E B7 E E B7 E
quick as a wink. You got - ta fill in the blanks; You got - ta
19 E B7sus B7 C#m E7/B A E E7
close your eyes and think. It was just like be - in' in a
who did Zac-che - us wan- na
2nd time to CODA
22 A E/B B7 E E/B
jail down in the bel - ly of the whale. (spoken) "Who
see from the top of the sy - ca-more
25 E E/B E B E A/B
was it?" "Jo - nah!" Up in a tree, in the

28
E B B7 E A/B E E7
top of a sy - ca-more tree, sat a lit - tle man on a
31
A B F#7/C# B/D# A/B E B7 E A/B
limb so high.___ He heard that (whoop!) would be pass - in' by. He
34
E7 A6 Amaj7 A E/G# F#m A6 B A/B
was so short that he could not see, And that's why he climbed up a
D. S. al CODA (to meas. 17)
CODA
37
E B7sus/E E E E/B E E/D B♭/C
sy - ca - more tree. You got - ta tree? (spoken) "Who was it?" "Je-sus!"
40
F C7 F F C7
Down in the den, in the bot - tom of the li - on's

43 F Bb/C F F7 Bb Bb/D
den, The king threw (whoop!) to the hun - gry beasts. The
46 C7 Bb/C A/C# C#o Dm
li - on's get - tin' read - y for a great big feast. They
48 F F7 Bb6 Am Gm7 Bb
smacked their mouths and they licked their paws, But
50 C Bb/C F C7sus/F F F C7
God closed their mouths and locked their jaws. You got - ta fill in the
53 F F/C F F C C#o Dm F7/C Bb
blanks; You got - ta close your eyes and think.

56 F F7 F7/C Bm7♭5 Bo F/C C7
Tell me now if you can, who was in the li - on's —
59 F F/C F F/C F F/A F7/A
den? (spoken) "Who was it?" "Dan-iel!" Who did Zac - che - us wan-na
62 B♭ B♭6 Bo F/C C7 F F/C
see from the top of the sy - ca-more tree, "Je-sus!"
65 F F7 B♭ B♭6 Bo F/C C7
Ev - 'ry - bod - y give a yell! Who was in the bel - ly of the
68 F F/C F C C7 F F/C F
whale? "Jo - nah!"

Father Abraham

TRADITIONAL

16
E♭
E♭/B♭
4.
E♭
arm, right foot. Fa - ther Lord, right arm, left arm, right foot, left
19
E♭
E♭/B♭
5.
E♭
foot. Fa - ther Lord, right arm, left arm, right foot, left
22
E♭
E♭/B♭
6.
E♭
foot, chin up. Fa - ther Lord, right arm, left arm, right foot, left
25
E♭
E♭/B♭
7.
E♭
foot, chin up, turn a - round. Fa - ther Lord, right arm, left
28
E♭
E♭6/9/B♭
E♭6
arm, right foot, left foot, chin up, turn a - round, sit down!

Every Day In Every Way

Words and Music by
HERB OWEN

10
1.
Dm7 G7 C C6/G Cmaj7 C6/G
love my Je - sus more!
13
2.
Dm7 G7 C G♭/A♭ A♭ D♭ B♭m/A♭ D♭maj7
love my Je - sus more! Ev - 'ry time I ask I find that
Take a look in - to the book and
15
D♭maj7 E♭m7 A♭7 E♭m E♭maj7/B♭ E♭m7
He will hear me when I pray. He is near me and will hear me
soon you'll start to un - der - stand all the glo - ry of the sto - ry:
17
E♭m7 A♭7 G♭/D♭ D♭ D♭ Fm/A♭ A♭m7
ev - 'ry min - ute, ev - 'ry day. How He un - der - stands I won - der,
God, the Son, be - came a man! You can be e - ter - nal - ly ex -

19
C♭/D♭ D♭ G♭ G♭ A♭9/G♭ Fm7 D°7
yet He loves me an - y - way! Ev - 'ry day in ev - 'ry way I
act - ly just what He has planned. Ev - 'ry day in ev - 'ry way I
21 1.
E♭m7 G♭maj7/A♭ A♭7 D♭ D♭6/A♭ D♭maj7 D♭6/A♭
love my Je - sus more!
24 2.
E♭m7 G♭maj7/A♭ A♭7 D♭ G/A A7 D A6/C♯
love my Je - sus more! Do you know He loves you so and
26
D/C G/B Gm6/B♭ A7 A9 Em+5
He has paid for all your sin? And He died, was cru - ci - fied and

28
Em7/A A7 Gm/D D D A7+5
on the third day rose a - gain! He will come to take us home to
30
Am7 C/D D7 G G A9/E Am6/F♯ B7
live for - ev - er - more with Him. Ev - 'ry day in ev - 'ry way I
32
Em7 A7 D G G♯o7 D/A B7♭9
love my Je - sus more! Ev - 'ry day in ev - 'ry way I
34
Em7 Gm/E Gmaj7/A A7 D D D/A D
love my Je - sus more!

How Did Moses Cross The Red Sea?

Words and Music by
HUGH MITCHELL

13
G
G
G/D
G
G/D
cross? Did he swim? No! No! Did he fly? No! No! Did he
16
G
F♯m/A
A7
Am7/D
D7
G
Cmaj7/G
G
D7/G
sail? No! No! No! No! Did he run? No! No! Did he
19
G
Cmaj7/G
G
A7
Ao7
A7
D7sus
D7
walk? No! No! How did he get a - cross? God
22
G
Bm7
C
Bm7sus
E7♭5/B♭
Am7
blew with His wind, puff, puff, puff, puff, He blew just e-nough, nough,

25 D D7/F♯ G/B D7/A G Am E/B Am/C Am7♭5
nough, nough, nough, and through the sea He made a —— path. That's
28 1. G/D C/D Bm/D D7 G Gmaj7 C/G C/D 2. G/D C/D Cmaj7/D D♯o7
how he got a - cross? How he got a -
31 Em Em/D C♯m7♭5 G/D C/D G/D G♯o7 Am E/B Cm6 Cm6/A
cross! And through the sea He made a —— path, that's
34 G/D Cm/D Cmaj7/D D7 G G/D G
how he got a - cross! ——

One Door And Only One

Second verse lyrics by
DIANE MAYFIELD

TRADITIONAL

10
Fm7 B♭7
1.
E♭ E♭/B♭ E♭ E♭/B♭ E♭ E♭/B♭ E♭ E♭/B♭
which side are you?
which side are
13
2.
E♭ E♭/B♭ E♭ E♭/B♭ F F/C F F/C
you?
15
F Fsus 2/4 Fmaj7 Fsus 2/4 F
One door, and on - ly one, and yet its sides are two,
17
B♭ Gm6 Am Dm7 F/G G7 Gm7 C7
"in - side" and "out - side," on which side are you?

19 F Fsus 2/4 Fmaj7 Fsus 2/4 F
One door, and on - ly one, and yet its sides are two,
21 B♭ Gm7 Am Dm7 Gm9 C7 F F/A
I'm on the in - side, on which side are you?
23 B♭ Gm6/B♭ Am7 Dm Gm9 Am7 B♭maj7 C7
I'm on the in - side, on which side are
25 F F/C F F/C F F/C F F/C F
you?

The Perfect 10

Words and Music by
KATHIE HILL & JANET McMAHAN

Slower, a tempo (♩ = 100)
16
A
Rall.
Dm Dm/A Dm Dm/A Dm Dm/A Dm Dm/A
"shalts" and "thou shalt nots."
19
Dm Dm/A Dm A7 A7/E A7 A7/E
Num - ber one we've just be - gun: — God should be first — in your life.
21
A7 A7/E A7 Dm A7
Num - ber two's the i - dol rule: — Those grav - en im - a - ges aren't nice.
23
Dm Dm/A Dm Dm/A Gm Gm/D Gm Gm/D
Num - ber three: God's name should be — nev - er spo - ken in jest.

25
Dm/A A Dm/B A7/C♯ Dm Dm
Num - ber four: the Sab - bath's for our wor - ship and for rest.
27
Gm Gm/D Gm Dm Dm/A Dm
Num - ber five: We all should strive to hon - or fa - ther and moth - er.
29
A A/E A7 Dm Dm/A D
Num - ber six: Don't get your kicks from kil - ling one — an - oth - er.
31
Gm Gm/D Gm Dm Dm/A Dm Dm/A
Num - ber sev - en: Life is heav - en when you're true — to your mate.

33
E7 E7/B E7 E7/B A A
Num-ber eight: Don't steal and break this rule for good-ness sake!
35
Dm Dm/A Dm A7 A7/E A7 A7/E
Num-ber nine: Don't be the kind — who goes a-round — tell-ing lies.
37
A7 A7/E A7 Dm A
Num-ber ten: Don't cov-et when you see your neigh-bor's house or wife.
39
Dm Dm/A Dm Dm/A Gm Gm/D Gm
That's the list and God in-sists we stay a-way — from these sins.
41
Dm/A A7 Dm D7
That is why we mem-o-rize com-mand-ments one through ten. The

43
Gm Gm/D Gm Dm Dm/A Dm
Per - fect Ten, The Per - fect Ten, they're
45
A7 A7/E A7 Dm Dm/A D Dsus/E D7/F♯
just as true as they were way back when God gave the
47
Gm Gm/D Gm Dm Dm/A Dm
Per - fect Ten, The Per - fect Ten. God
49
1.
A7 Dm Dm/A D Dsus/E D7/F♯
gave The Per - fect Ten. The
51
2.
A A♯o7 Dm6/B A7/C♯ Dm Dm/A Dm Dm/A Dm Dm/A Dm A Dm
gave The Per - fect Ten!

Isn't It Grand To Be A Christian

Words and Music by
CHARLOTTE McCROSSAN

7
B♭ E♭/B♭ B♭ B♭/A Gm7
grand to be a Christ-ian, Mon-day, Tues-day, Wednes-day, Thurs-day, Fri-day,
9
Cm7sus F Cm F7
1.
B♭ Gm Cm7sus Cm7sus/F
Sat-ur-day, and all day Sun-day, is-n't it grand! Is-n't it
11
2.
B♭ B♭/A G7sus C C♯o7 Dm Fmaj7/G G7
grand! Is-n't it grand to be a Christ-ian, is-n't it
13
C Csus2 4/D D♯o C/E F Fmaj7 F♯o7
grand! Is-n't it grand to be a Christ-ian, is-n't it

15 C/G G/F C6/E Dm7 G7 C Dm7
grand! Is - n't it grand to be a Christ - ian, Mon - day,
17 C/E F C/G Eo7 C#o7 Dm Fmaj7/G G7
Tues - day, Wednes-day, Thurs-day, Fri - day Sat - ur - day, and all day Sun - day, is - n't it
19 C C/B Am7 Dm7sus Dm7/G G7
grand! Is - n't it grand to be a Christ - ian, is - n't it
21 Am Am7 C#o7 Dm Fmaj7/G G7 C C/G C
grand! Is - n't it grand to be a Christ-ian, is - n't it grand!

"Abundawonderful" Life In Jesus

Words and Music by
KATHIE HILL

10
Eb Eb/Bb Eb Eb/G Gbo7 Bb7/F Bb9
Him. Je - sus gives a rea - son for
Je - sus gives you life ev - er -
12
Eb Bb7 Fm7 Bb7
liv - ing, Je - sus gives you joy when you are
last - ing, Je - sus gives you love when you're a -
14
Eb Eb/Bb Eb Cm7 F7
sad. He gives hope when days are drear - y,
lone. He gives peace when you are wor - ried,
16
Bb/D Gm F7 Cm7 Cm7/F F7
strength when you are wear - y. He can make life cheer - y ev - en
pa - tience when you're hur - ried. When your day is blur - ry, He is

18 B♭7sus B♭ B♭7 A♭maj7/B♭ B♭7 (Repeat twice)
when things look bad! There is a
still in con - trol!
20 CODA E♭ Cm Cm7 Fm7 A♭maj7/B♭ B♭7
Him, There's a - bun - da - won - der - ful life in
22 E♭ Cm Cm7 Fm7 Fm9
Him. There's a - bun - da - won - der - ful life
24 A♭maj7/B♭ B♭ E♭ E♭/B♭ E♭6 E♭/B♭ E♭ E♭/B♭ E♭ B♭ E♭
in Him!

Behold, Behold!

TRADITIONAL

14 D(2) D F#7sus/C# F#7/C# B7sus B B7 E7 D/E E/D
voice, If an - y boy hear my voice, and will
17 A/C# E A A#o7 Bm
1. D/E E E7 A F#m7 Bm E7sus
o - pen, o - pen, o - pen the door, I will come in. Be -
21 2. A/E E#o7 F#m F#m/C# C#m7 B F#m7/C# B7/D# B7
will come in. I will
24 E E9/B C#m/E E7 A A/E A A/E A
come in.

I Have Decided To Follow Jesus

TRADITIONAL

12
C Cmaj7 C6/G Cmaj7/G C Cmaj7/G C7 B♭/D C7/E
ren - dered my all to Je - sus, I have sur -
world but give me the Sav - ior, Take the whole
14
F C6/E Dm7 F6/G F/G C9 Fmaj9
ren - dered my all to Je - sus, I have sur - ren - dered my all to
world but give me the Sav - ior, Take the whole world but give me the
17
E7 Am F C/G C+/G Fmaj7/G G7
1.
C F6/G
Je - sus, No turn-ing back, No turn-ing back! Take the whole
Sav - ior, No turn-ing back, No turn-ing
20
2.
Am Fmaj7 C/G Cmaj7/G Dm7/G G7 F C
back! No turn - ing back, No turn - ing back!

I've Been Redeemed

ANONYMOUS

16
E♭7 E♭7/G D♭/F E♭7 A♭ A♭/E♭ A♭ B♭/A♭ A♭
I've been re - deemed by the blood of the Lamb, I'm go - ing
God sent His Son to die for me so I could
19
E♭ G/D Cm Cm7 Fm Fm sus 2/4 Fm7 Gm/B♭ B♭7
to the prom - ised land. All my sins are washed a - way, I've been re -
live e - ter - nal - ly.
23
1.
E♭ E♭7/G A♭ E♭ E♭ D/B♭ E♭/B♭
deemed! God sent His
2.
E♭ E♭7/G A♭ E♭
deemed!
26
E♭/B♭ E♭ E F F7/A B♭ B♭7 F F E/C F/C
You can talk a - bout

29
F F/A B♭ Gm7 F E/C F/C F F7/A B♭ Gm7
me just all you please,
way to heav'n a - bove,
32
F C7/F F Gm Am7 B♭6 C B♭/C C7
You can talk a - bout me just all you
I'm on my way to heav'n a -
35
F Fmaj7/C F7 E♭/F F7 B♭ B♭/F
please. You can talk a - bout me just all you
bove, I'm on my way to heav'n a -
38
B♭ C C7/E F A/E Dm Dm7
please, I'll talk a - bout you down on my knees.
bove, I'm filled with God's fan - tas - tic love. All my

41 Gm Gm sus 2/4 Gm7 Am/C C7
1. F F7/A B♭ B♭7 F
sins are washed a - way, I've been re - deemed!
44 F E/C F/C
2. F F7/A B♭ B♭7 F F/E Dm Dm/C
I'm on my deemed! All my
47 Gm/B♭ Gm Gm sus 2/4 B♭/C Am/C C♯o7 Dm
sins are washed a - way, I've been re - deemed!
50 F7sus/C F7 Gm/B♭ D7sus/A Gm7 Am/C C7 F B♭ F
All my sins are washed a - way, I've been re - deemed!

Wisdom

Words and Music by
HERB OWEN

13
2.
F F/A B♭ C F B♭ Gm B♭maj7
Hear now ye chil - dren the
16
C F Am//E Dm Fmaj7/C
wis - dom of God; I teach you
19
Gm/B♭ Gm Gm7 C C7 F F/A B♭ C
well so for - sake not my law.
22
F Fmaj7 B♭ Gm Gm9 C
Wis - dom is see - ing the world as God

25
F Am7/E Dm F7sus/C F7/C Gm/B♭ G/B G7/B
sees, Do - ing what He does so
28
C C7 F C/D G G/B
Him I can please. In the word of God
31
C Am7 C D D7 C/D D7 G G/B C D
treas - ures there I find,
34
G Bm7 G/B C C#7♭5 C#o7 D7 C/D D7 G
un - der - stand - ing for my heart and know - ledge for my mind.

37 G G/B C D G Bm7 G/B C Am7
CHOIR 2
Hear now — ye chil - dren — the
CHOIR 1
God has prom-ised me
40 D7 Am7 D7 G D7sus G Bm7 G/B
wis - dom — of God; I teach — you
wis - dom from a - bove; I will have suc -
43 C G6/B Am7 D C/D D7 G G/B C D
well, so — for - sake not — my law.
cess if un - der - stand - ing I will love.

46
G Bm7 G/B C Am7 Bm C D7 C/D D7
Wis dom — is see - ing — the world as — God
If I choose to make wis - dom my life's
49
G C D Em Dm7 G7/D A/C# Cm6
sees, Do - ing — what He does — so
goal. He will then re - ward me with — much
52
D C/D D7 G G/B C D G Bm7 G/B
Him I — can please.
ALL
hon - or as I grow. Don't let me for - get —

55
C Am7 D7 C/D D7 G G/B
les - sons I have learned.
58
Em Dm7 G7/D A/C# Cm6 D C/D D D7 G
Keep them all with - in my heart as to them I re - turn.
61
(G) G/B C D Em D6 G6/D C G6/B Am7 C#o7
Keep them all with - in my heart as
64
D C/D D7 G
to them I re - turn.

See The Work Of The Lord

Words and Music by
STEVE & JILL GROSSMAN
RICKY & TRISHA BLAIR

13 C F C G G7
God com - mand - ed the world — to be, — see the work — of the
16 C2 C Cmaj7/G C/G C G7/D C/E C F Em7 Am
Lord. Fish and birds, sand and sea, —
19 Dm F/G G7 C
see the work — of the Lord.
21 F C Am Dm7 Em/G G7
Sun - light, — moon - bright, — all things — for

24 C Dm/C C C/E F Em7 A7♭9
His de - light. God made the whole world,
2nd time to CODA
27 Dm7 G9 G7 C Dm7 G7sus G7
see the work of the Lord.
30 C F C Dm7 G7
Da - vid killed him a gi - ant man, see the work of the
33 C Am7 Dm7 G7 C C/E C F/A F C
Lord. When oth - er men doubt Da - vid know, God can,

36 Dm7 F/G G7 C F/C G/C C
see the work — of the Lord. Dan - iel put in the
39 F C/E C G G7 C C#o7 Dm7 G7
Li - on's den, — see the work — of the Lord. When
42 C7 F Em7 A7 Dm7 F/G G7
morn - ing come old Dan - iel He grin, — see the work — of the
45 C
Lord.
D. S. al CODA
(to meas. 21)
CODA
C Dm7 C/E F G9/F G7/F
Lord. Oh, — Sun - light, —

48
Em7 Am Am7 Dm7 Em/G G7 C G7/D C/E C
moon - bright, all things for His de - light.
51
F G9/F Em7♭5 A7 Dm7 F/G G7
God made the whole world, see the work of the
54
C Am Am7 Dm7 G9 G7 C A7♭9
Lord. See the work of the Lord.
57
Dm7 F/G G7 C
See the work of the Lord.

Happy All The Time

Words and Music by
A. B. SIMPSON

9
D/F♯ A9/E D♯o7
1.
Em A7 D D/A
in - right, out - right, up - right, down - right, hap - py all the time! I'm
11
2.
Em A7 D D/C B♭7sus B♭7 A♭/C B♭7/D
hap - py all the time! I'm
14
E♭ Gm Cm7 Fm Fm+5 Fm7/B♭ B♭7
in - right, out - right, up - right, down-right, hap - py all the time, I'm
16
Fm Fm maj7 C Fm7 B♭9 E♭/B♭ B♭7 E♭2 E♭
in - right, out - right, up - right, down-right, hap - py all the time. Since

18
E♭7
D♭/E♭
E♭7/G
A♭
Am7♭5
A°7
Je - sus Christ came in and cleansed my heart from sin, I'm
20
E♭/B♭
B♭7/A♭
E♭6/G
Cm7
Fm7
B♭7
E♭
F♯°7
in - right, out - right, up - right, down-right, hap - py all the time. I'm
22
E♭/G
B♭7/F
E♭6
E°7
Fm7
A♭maj7
F
B♭7
in - right, out - right, up - right, down - right, hap - py all the
24
E♭
E♭/B♭
E♭
B♭7
E♭
time!

Rolled Away

TRADITIONAL

12 A♭(2) A♭ A♭7/C D♭ E♭/D♭ D♭ E♭9/B♭ A♭/C A°7 B♭m E♭7
go 'neath the crim - son flow, hal - le - lu - jah! Rolled a -
15 A♭ B♭m7 Cm Cm7 Fm A♭7/E♭
1. D♭6 B♭m7 D♭/E♭ E♭7
way, rolled a-way, rolled a - way. Ev - 'ry bur - den of my heart rolled a -
18 A♭ B♭m7 B°7 A♭/C
2. D♭6 B♭7/D D♭/E♭ E♭7
way! Ev - 'ry bur - den of my heart rolled a -
20 Fm E♭m7 A♭7 D♭6 B♭7/D D♭/E♭ E♭7 D♭/A♭ A♭
way. Ev - 'ry bur - den of my heart rolled a - way.

The Floating Zoo

Words and Music by
JANET McMAHAN WILSON & TED WILSON

17
C G/B Am7 G C D G G/D
big mouthed frogs and the pup - py dogs, two by two.
21
G
3.
C G/B Am7 G C G/B
sailed a - way on a rain - y day, with the cats and the bats and the
25
Am7 G C G/B Am7 G C D
long tailed rats, the big mouthed frogs and the pup - py dogs, two by
29
G G/D G
4.
C G/B Am7 G
two. sailed a - way on a rain - y day, with the

33
C G/B Am7 G C G/B
mice and the moose and the kan - ga - roos, the cats and the bats and the
36
Am7 G C G/B Am7 G C D
long tailed rats, the big mouthed frogs and the pup - py dogs, two by
40
G G/F E♭7 D♭/F E♭7/G A♭ A♭/C D♭ B♭
two. No - ah cried, "Come on, crit - ters,
44
E♭ A♭ A♭6/9
1.
D♭ A♭/C
all a - board for the float - ing zoo." So they sailed a - way on a

48
Bbm7 Ab Db Ab/C Bbm7 Ab
rain - y day, with the el - e - phants and the pel - i - cans, the
51
Db Ab/C Bbm7 Ab Db Ab/C
mice and the moose and the kan - ga - roos, the cats and the bats and the
54
Bbm7 Ab Db Ab/C Bbm7 Ab Db Eb
long tailed rats, the big mouthed frogs and the pup - py dogs, two by
58
Ab Ab/Eb Ab
two.
2.
Db Ab/C Bbm7 Ab
sailed a - way on a rain - y day, with the

62
Db Ab/C Bbm7 Ab Db Ab/C
hon - ey bees and the chim - pan - zees, the el - e - phants and the
65
Bbm7 Ab Db Ab/C Bbm7 Ab
pel - i - cans, the mice and the moose and the kan - ga - roos, the
68
Db Ab/C Bbm7 Ab Db Ab/C
cats and the bats and the long tailed rats, the big mouthed frogs and the
71
Bbm7 Ab Db Eb Ab Ab/Eb Ab
pup - py dogs two by two.

75 3. D♭ A♭/C B♭m7 A♭ D♭ A♭/C
sailed a - way on a rain - y day, the big and the small, he
78 B♭m7 A♭ D♭ A♭/C B♭m7 A♭
called them all, the hon - ey bees and the chim - pan - zees, the
81 D♭ A♭/C B♭m7 A♭ D♭ A♭/C
el - e - phants and the pel - i - cans, the mice and the moose and the
84 B♭m7 A♭ D♭ A♭/C B♭m7 A♭
kan - ga - roos, the cats and the bats and the long tailed rats, the

87
D♭ A♭/C B♭m7 A♭ D♭ E♭ A♭ A♭/E♭
big mouthed frogs and the pup - py dogs, two by two.
91
A♭ A♭ A♭/C D♭ B♭ E♭
No - ah cried, "Come on, crit - ters, all a - board for the
95
A♭ A♭6/9 D♭ A♭/C B♭m7 A♭
float - ing zoo." So they sailed a - way on a rain - y day,
99
D♭ E♭ A♭6
two by two.

Come And Go With Me

TRADITIONAL

12 G C C/E G D6/F♯ Em A/C♯ Cm6
Come and go with me to my Fa-ther's house, to my Fa-ther's house,
15 D C/E D/F♯ G Cmaj7 G B7/F♯ Em G7/D
to my Fa - ther's house. Come and go with me
17 C C♯o7 G/D A13/9 A9 Am7/D D♯o7 Em Em/C♯
to my Fa-ther's house where there's joy, joy, joy. Where there's
20 Cmaj7/D D Cmaj7 Am7/G D7 C Bm Am7 G
joy, joy, joy.

Creature Praise

Words and Music by
DAVID MATTHEWS

10
Ab/C Cb7 Eb/Bb Ab/Bb Eb
hot and cold crea - tures, come now and praise the Lord.
12
Eb/Bb Eb/C Eb/D Eb Eb/Bb Ab/Eb Eb Eb/Bb Eb7
Sing praise to the Fa - ther, sing
15
Ab Ab/Eb Ab Eb Eb/Bb Eb/C Eb/D Eb Eb/Bb
praise to the Son, sing praise to the
18
Ab/Eb Eb Eb/Bb Cm7 F7 Bb7
Spir - it Who makes all crea - tures one. Sing

21
Eb Eb/Bb Ab/Eb Eb Eb7/Bb Ab
praise for the good - ness — of what the Lord has —
24
Abm Abm6/Cb Eb/Bb Cm Fm7sus Ab/Bb Eb
done. Let all crea - tures praise — the Lord!
27
1.
Eb Eb/C Eb/Bb Eb Gm7 F#m7 Fm7 Ab/Bb
2.
Eb Eb/Bb Eb Eb/D
30
Cm Cm/Bb Cm/A Eb/Bb Cm Fm7sus Ab/Bb Eb
Let all crea - tures praise the Lord!
33
Eb Gm7 F#m7 Fm7 Ab/Bb Eb Eb/Bb

A-B-C-D-E-F-G
(The Alphabet Chorus)

Words and Music by
HUGH MITCHELL

15 Gm9 Am7 B♭6 Dm C7/E Gm7/D C7 Gm/F F F/C
S T U, I be - lieve God's word is true;
18 F F7 B♭ Gm7 Am7 Dm7
U V dou - ble U, God has prom-ised you, X Y Z, A
21 1. Gm9 C7 F F/C
home e - ter - nal - ly.
2. Gm7 E° Dm Am/C
home e - ter - nal - ly.
24 B♭maj9 C/B♭ Am7♭5 D7 G7sus G7 Gm7/C C7 F F/C F
X Y Z, A home e - ter - nal - ly.

Wonderful To Be In The Family Of God

Words and Music by
HERB OWEN

10
Cm Ebmaj7/Bb Ab Bb Eb
won - der - ing just what to do, how great it is to praise Him and say:—
tell the world He loves them so and work to - geth - er in one ac - cord.—
12
Eb Db/Eb Eb7 Ab Fm7 Bb7
Don't cha know it's won - der - ful to be in the
14
Eb Bb/D Cm Fm7 Bb7sus Bb7
fam - 'ly of God,— im - pos - si - ble to count all the
16
Eb Fm7 F#o Eb/G Ab Eb/G Eb
bless - ings He's giv - en; Re - mark - a - ble to know
18
Ab Eb/G Cm Fm Fm/Eb Bb7/D Bb7
that He loves us so, and com - fort - ing He's pa - tient as we

20 E♭ B♭ E♭ E♭/G A♭ E♭/G E♭
learn and grow; Awe - some just to see His
22 B♭9/F E°7
1. Fm7 B♭7
love for you and me, and glo - ri - ous that we are His e -
24 E♭ A♭/B♭ E♭
2. Fm7 B♭7
ter - nal - ly! glo - ri - ous that we are His e -
26 E♭ E♭/D Cm E°7 Fm7 B♭7
ter - nal - ly! And glo - ri - ous that we are His e -
28 E♭ A♭/E♭ A♭ E♭ B♭/D E♭ B♭7 E♭
ter - nal - ly!

Everybody Ought To Know

TRADITIONAL

13 F F6 Fmaj7 F6 F F/E♭
know, ev - 'ry - bod - y ought to know,
16 D9 D7♭9 G F(2)/A G/B C Gm Am/C C7
ev - 'ry - bod - y ought to know who Je - sus
19 F F/A B♭ Gm7 F Gm/F F/C B♭6/C F Fmaj7/C
is. He's the
22 Cm7/F F7 B♭ F/A Gm7 C9 F
lil - ly of the val - ley, He's the

26
F Dm7 Gm7 Gm7/D C7 B♭/D C7/E F Fmaj7/C
bright and morn - ing star. He's the
30
Cm9 F7 B♭2 B♭ Bm7♭5 Bo F/C Dm7
fair - est of ten thou - sand, ev - 'ry -
34
B♭maj7 Am7 Gm7 C7 F B♭/F
Ev - 'ry - bod - y ought to
bod - y ought to know.
37
F F6 Fmaj7 F6
know, ev - 'ry - bod - y ought to
ev - 'ry - bod - y ought to know,

39
F
Cm6/E♭
D7
D+
D7
know,
ev - 'ry-bod - y ought to
ev - 'ry-bod - y ought to know,
41
Gm
Am/G
Gm7
Am/G
Gm7
Am/C
C7
1.
F
know,
who Je - sus is.
ev - 'ry-bod - y ought to know who Je - sus is.
44
B♭/F
2.
B♭
F/A
Gm7
F
Ev - 'ry-bod - y ought to
is.
is.

He L-O-V-E-S Me

Words and Music by
JANET & TED WILSON

11
D
Em
A7
He gave His L - I - F - E as a G - I -
He'll give you L - I - F - E as a G - I -
13
F#m7
B7
B7sus/C#
B7/D#
Em
A7
F - T just for M - E, Now I want to T - E - L - L all the
F - T and you'll S - E - E, You'll
15
D D/A D D/A D D/A D D#o7
Em7 Em A7
world.
He L - O - V - E - S M - E, He
18
F#m7
B7
Em
A
A7
L - O - V - E - S M - E, Yes, I know J - E - S - U - S L -

20
D D/A D D/A D D#o7 Em7 Em A7
O - V - E - S me. He said He L - O - V - E - S M - E, He
23
F#m7 B7 Em7 A7
L - O - V - E - S M - E, and I know He L - O - V - E - S
25
1.
Em7 A7 D D/A D Em7 D/F# D Em/D D
to meas. 7
2.
Em7 A7
Y - O - U, too. If you will Y - O - U,
29
D Bm Bm7
Repeat Chorus
3.
Em7 A7 D D/A D D/A D D/A D
too. He loves — you, too.

Everybody Ought To Love Jesus

Words and Music by
HARRY DIXON LOES

13
B♭7sus B♭7 A♭/C B♭7/D
E♭ Gm7 A♭maj7 B♭9/A♭ Gm7 E°7
Ev - 'ry-bod - y ought to keep smil - ing,
16
Fm7 B♭7/D B♭7
E♭2 E♭ E♭9 E♭7/G
A♭ B♭9/F Gm7 Cm
smil - ing, smil - ing; If you have a lit - tle frown
19
B°7 Cm/B♭
A♭ A♭m E♭6/B♭
Fm7/E♭ B♭/D E♭ E♭7/G
turn it up - side down, ev - 'ry-bod - y ought to keep smil - ing.
22
A♭ G7 Cm E♭7/B♭
A♭6 A♭6/C B♭ A♭/C B♭/D
E♭sus E♭sus/B♭
E♭
Ev - 'ry-bod - y ought to keep smil - ing.

Hal-Le-La-Le-La-Le-Lu-Jah

Words and Music by
JANET McMAHAN WILSON & TED WILSON

3rd time to CODA
10
Gm Gm/D Gm Dm Dm/A Dm
Lift your voice, re - joice and sing Hal - le - la - le - la - le - lu - jah,
12
A D Dm/A Dm Dm/A Dm Dm/A D Dsus/E D/F♯
to the King of Kings!
15
Gm C7 F B♭ Gm/E A7+5 A7
He is the Ho - ly One, Je - sus, God's
18
Dm Dm sus/E D/F♯ Gm C7
on - ly Son, crown - ing glo - ry of

20
F Dm E7
all crea - a - tion, clap your hands in cel - e -
22
D. S. 2 times al CODA
CODA
A A Dm
bra - tion! to the King of Kings.
24
A A Gm/B♭ Dm6/B A7/C♯
Hal - le - la - le - la - le - lu - jah to the King of
26
Dm Dm/A Dm Dm/A Dm Dm/A Dm A Dm
Kings!

Every Promise In The Book Is Mine

TRADITIONAL

11 2.
Eb Bb6/D Bb/C C7 F F/E Dm7 G7
mine. Ev - 'ry prom - ise in the Book is
13
Gm7 C7 Gm7 Gm7b5 C7
mine, Ev - 'ry chap - ter, ev - 'ry verse, ev - 'ry
15
F Dm7 Gm9 C7b9 Cm7 F7
line; all are bless - ings of His love di -
17
Bb Bb/A Gm7b5 Bbm6/Db F/C Gm7/C C#o7
vine, Ev - 'ry prom - ise in the Book is
19
Dm F7/C Bb Eb9 F6/C Gm C7 Fsus F
mine, Ev - 'ry prom - ise in the Book is mine.

Take A Step Of Faith

Words and Music by
KATHIE HILL

16 Dm7 G7 C Am7 D7 C6/E D9 G7sus G7 F/A G7/B C C/G G7
front of your face, Take a step of faith. With no star to
20 C C7 F F/C C F Dm7 G7/D C F/C
guide your way,— God's still be - side you say - ing, "Take a step of
24 C G/B Am
1. D9 Fmaj7/G G7 C F/C C G F/A G/B
faith, just take a step of faith."
28
2. D9 Fmaj7/G G♯o7 Am F G C F/C C7 Fmaj7
take a step of faith. Take a step of faith, just
32 D9 C6/E D9/F♯ D9 Fmaj7/G G7 C
take a step of faith."

The Wise Man And The Foolish Man

TRADITIONAL

10 F F B♭/F F Am/C C7 Gm7
down. The rains came down and the floods came up. The
13 C7 Am/C C7 Gm/F F F/C F D7+5 D7
rains came down and the floods came up, The rains came down and the
16 F/G Gm Gm7
1. C Gm7 Cm6 C7 F
floods came up, and the house on the rock stood fast!
19 F
2. Slowing
C Gm7 B♭maj7/C C7 F
The house on the sand went smash! (shouted)

I Want To Be A Little Lighthouse

Words and Music by
JAMES L. Mc KEE

10 C6/E C/E Am Am7 Dm7 G7 C G7
I can be a light - house if I let Him shine thru me. I want to
12 C Dm7 C/E D7 G7sus G7
be a lit - tle light - house for the Lord, I want to
14 Dm G7 F/G G7 C F/C C G7
be a lit - tle light - house for the Lord. I want to
16 C Cmaj7 C7 F C/E Dm7 Dm7♭5
shine my light so oth - ers can see to climb on board, I want to
D. S. al CODA
18 C/G Am7 Dm7 G7 C F C/E G7
be a lit - tle light - house for the Lord. When

CODA
20 C/E Am Dm7 G7 C C/B♭ G♭/A♭
be a lit - tle light - house and shine out in - to the night. Poor
23 D♭ D♭/F G♭ G♭6 D♭
Dan - iel was sup - posed to be the li - on's meal one night, but
25 D♭ B♭m B♭m7 E♭7 A♭7 G♭/B♭ A♭13/C
God kept all their mouths shut so they could - n't take a bite. I
27 D♭ D♭maj7/A♭ D♭7 G♭ E♭m7 D♭2/F D♭/F
want to pray like Dan - iel did and please God ev - 'ry day, and
29 D♭ G♭/D♭ D♭ B♭m7 E♭m7 A♭7 D♭
be a lit - tle light-house so my friends can see the way. I want to

31
D♭ D♭/C B♭m7 E♭7 A♭7sus A♭
be a lit - tle light - house for the Lord. I want to
33
E♭m E♭m7/B♭ G♭/A♭ A♭7 D♭ D♭sus D♭
be a lit - tle light - house for the Lord. I want to
35
D♭ D♭maj7 D♭7 G♭ D♭/F G♭m6/E♭ G♭m6
shine my light so oth - ers can see to climb on board, I want to
37
D♭/A♭ A♭7sus A♭7 Gm7♭5 G♭m7 G♭m6/E♭
be a lit - tle light - house for the Lord. I want to
39
D♭/A♭ A♭7sus A♭7 D♭ D♭/A♭ D♭
be a lit - tle light - house for the Lord.

My Heart Is Steadfast

Words and Music by
BRIAN CARR & ED KEE

15 Dm C/E Dm/F F Gsus G C
I will not be moved. My heart is
18 F/C C F G/F F C/E
stead - fast, what He does in me will last.
21 Dm7 C/E Dm/F C/G Am Dm F6/G F/G
My heart is stead - fast, I will not be
24 1. C F/C Fmaj7/C G/C
moved.

27 F/C C G7/C C C/G
2. C Gb/Ab Ab Db
moved. My heart — is
30 Ebm7 Db/F Gb Ab/Gb Gb Db/F
stead - fast, what He does in me — will last. —
33 Gb/Eb Db/F Ebm/Gb Db/Ab Bbm Ebm Bbm/Eb Ebm/Gb Gb
My heart — is stead - fast, — I will not — be
36 Absus Ab Absus Ab Db Gb/Db Db
moved. My heart — is stead - fast, —

39
Gb Ab/Gb Gb Db/F Gb/Eb Db/F Gb
what He does in me will last. My heart is
42
Db/Ab Bbm Ebm Gbmaj7 Absus Gb/Ab Db Db/C Bbm Bbm/Db
stead - fast, I will not be moved.
45
Ebm Db/F Gb Gb/Ab Db
I will not be moved.
48
Gb/Db Ab/Db Gb/Db Db Ebm/Ab Db

Stand Up For Jesus

Words and Music by
JAN ESTERLINE,
JANET McMAHAN WILSON & TED WILSON

10
Eb Eb/Bb Eb Eb/Bb Ab Abm6
heart. Lift your voic - es to the
13
Eb Ab Abm6 Eb Eb/G Eb
sky yi! For He is for - ev - er - more the Lord most high!
16
Ab G Cm Abm6/Cb Eb/Bb Cm F7
Clap your hands, re - joice and sing, for we be - long to the
D. S. al CODA
CODA
19
Bb7sus Bb7 Bbo Bb7 Eb Cm Cm7
King! Stand heart.
22
Fm Eo7 Fm/Eb Co7 Bb7sus Ab/Bb Bb7 Eb Ab Fm7 Eb
ev - 'ry - bod - y stand up for Je - sus!